THE BAT BOY & HIS VIOLIN

THE BAT BOY & HIS VIOLIN

By GAVIN CURTIS

Illustrated by E. B. LEWIS

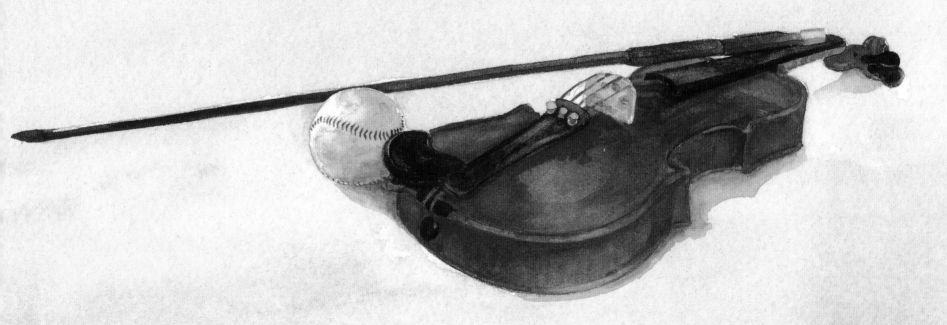

Center for the Collaborative Classroom

This Center for the Collaborative Classroom edition is reprinted by arrangement
with Simon & Schuster Books for Young Readers,
an imprint of Simon & Schuster Children's Publishing Division.

Designed by Paul Zakris
The text for this book was set in 17-point Baskerville Book.
The illustrations were rendered in watercolor.

Center for the Collaborative Classroom
1001 Marina Village Parkway, Suite 110
Alameda, CA 94501
800.666.7270 * fax: 510.464.3670
collaborativeclassroom.org

ISBN 978-1-61003-618-4
Printed in China

2 3 4 5 6 7 8 9 10 RRD 22 21 20 19 18 17

In memory of Mrs. Daisy D. Hooper,
whose music still chases away my jitters.
—G. C.

To the heroes of the Negro Leagues.
—E. B. L.

I sashay my bow across the violin strings the way a mosquito skims a summer pond. With hardly any mistakes, Tchaikovsky fills the living room of our house on Tyler Road. When the back door slams and metal cleats stomp onto the kitchen floor, I know Papa is home.

"Is—Reginald—at—it—again?" he shouts between notes.

"Hush up," Mama says, "I just love this one."

"Cooped up inside all the time, it's a wonder that boy don't sprout mushrooms."

I try to play louder than Papa's voice by sawing the music hard. He sometimes comes home in a bad mood because he's the manager of the Dukes—the worst team in the Negro National League. So far, the 1948 season has been the toughest yet. Papa's even having trouble booking games the team is likely to lose. He says it's because all his best hitters and fielders are going over to play for white teams, the way Jackie Robinson did last year.

"You know our baby wants to be in a famous orchestra someday," Mama says, following Papa into the living room.

"Well, right now the Dukes could use a bat boy, and I think it'll do Reginald some good to get out the house. We'll get him a uniform and everything."

I stop playing. "What about my practice?" I ask. "Don't you remember I have a recital next month in the basement at church?"

"You can rehearse 'tween innings. Tendin' to bats don't take up no whole lotta time." Papa pretends to swing one at an invisible pitch. "Anyway, you do a good job and I'll let you have your fiddle recital right here."

I smile because our living room is bigger than the church basement. "I prefer to call it a violin," I say.

Papa doesn't hear. He's too busy admiring the trophy cabinet. "Heck," Papa says, "this might even inspire you to become a ball player the way your ol' man was."

The next morning, I ride with Papa and the Dukes to Cleveland
on the team's rickety old bus. We get to the field for our game
against the Buckeyes, and the bleachers are already packed with
their fans.

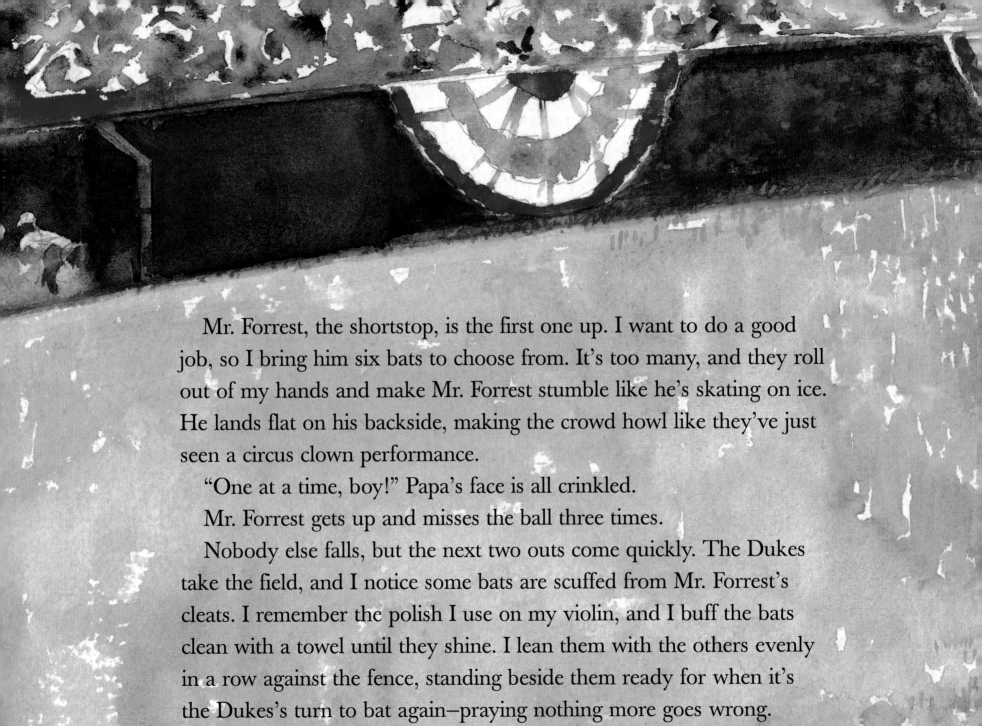

Mr. Forrest, the shortstop, is the first one up. I want to do a good job, so I bring him six bats to choose from. It's too many, and they roll out of my hands and make Mr. Forrest stumble like he's skating on ice. He lands flat on his backside, making the crowd howl like they've just seen a circus clown performance.

"One at a time, boy!" Papa's face is all crinkled.

Mr. Forrest gets up and misses the ball three times.

Nobody else falls, but the next two outs come quickly. The Dukes take the field, and I notice some bats are scuffed from Mr. Forrest's cleats. I remember the polish I use on my violin, and I buff the bats clean with a towel until they shine. I lean them with the others evenly in a row against the fence, standing beside them ready for when it's the Dukes's turn to bat again—praying nothing more goes wrong.

11

"Startin' to get the hang of it, ain't ya," Papa says.

"Yep," I say, rocking heel to toe and toe to heel.

Mr. Mosley, the third baseman, tips his cap because I hand him a bat. When he swings at the pitch, the bat slips out of his hand and misses the umpire's head by no more than an inch.

"I'll pass out the bats," Papa says after the umpire has calmed down. Papa grumbles under his breath because the umpire makes him rub dirt on each bat.

"Can I help?" I ask.

"Why don't you relax a spell on the bench. It'll give you a chance to fiddle."

"You mean violin."

"Just keep it low. Lord knows I don't need nothing makin' my headache worse." Papa takes his cap off and uses it to wipe the sweat from his face.

I play *Swan Lake* the way I feel—sad and quiet. But I'm not clumsy with my violin. I'm careful, glancing only one time at the music I know by heart. In the last measure, I pull my bow slowly to hold the final note long.

"That sure was somethin' pretty," says Mr. LaRue, the center fielder who is waiting on deck. "Kinda makes the hairs on the back of my neck do a jig."

"Thank you," I say, a little embarrassed that anyone had listened.

"You're up, LaRue," Papa calls. His headache must have disappeared, because a smile crosses his face. "How 'bout doin' a *jig* with that bat and getting a hit?"

As Mr. LaRue steps up to the plate, I start to play again. He lets the first pitch go past him but swings hard on the next.

"RUN!" Papa yells because Mr. LaRue sends the ball toward the outfield.

Before he can reach first base, the ball leaves the park. He takes his time and does a kind of hop around the field while I play until he gets back to home plate.

Mr. Ervin, the catcher, bats next, and I play Mozart—and the same thing happens again. It happens with the left fielder, the second baseman, and the third baseman, too.

I'm bushed by the ninth inning, but the Dukes have beaten the Buckeyes, seven to four. It's the first game they win in months.

"Ain't this a talented boy," Papa says, and massages *my* arm instead of the pitcher's.

Each day, I like being the bat boy more than the last. Papa handles the bats, and he lets me play my violin as much as I want. Besides that, the Dukes have stopped losing. I haven't seen Papa this happy since he was a player.

Three weeks into our winning streak, Papa makes an important announcement. "We got us a game with the Monarchs!"

I'm the only one not cheering, so I ask, "Are they any good?"

"Any good?" he says. "Why, they're the best colored team there is."

"I thought *we* were," I say.

"If we beat them Monarchs, we will be. Folks are sayin' now that baseball's becoming integrated, the Negro Leagues won't be 'round forever. The season's coming to an end, and this might be the Dukes's last chance to make a real mark—make a name for ourselves." Papa lifts me up onto his shoulder. "Good thing we got us a gifted little bat boy."

The night before the big game, Papa can't find a hotel in town that will accept the Dukes. "We don't exactly cotton to coloreds sleepin' in our beds," one white clerk says. "Y'all gonna have to look elsewheres."

"Thank you kindly just the same," Papa says, tipping his cap. "I reckon our bus will do us fine."

We park on a field outside the stadium, and Mr. LaRue grills catfish and corn on the cob. After dinner, fancying their chances of winning a pennant makes the team too jittery to sleep, so I play them a lullaby Mama sometimes hums to me before bed.

"Reginald," Papa says when the sound of snores joins the sound of crickets, "you got a knack. That fool clerk should have heard your pretty fiddlin'."

"*Violining*," I tell Papa before falling asleep on his belly.

The next day, the sun is high and little shade can be found once the game has gone into extra innings. I play my best, but nothing seems to work—at least not for the Dukes. I play Beethoven, and Mr. Forrest and Mr. Mosley both hit balls that seem to fly right back into the pitcher's glove. I play Mozart, and Mr. LaRue is tagged out at home. But when I play Bach with the game tied, two outs and Papa very nervous, Mr. O'Neil from the Monarchs knocks a high, curling wallop into deep left field. I stop playing just in time to see the ball easily clear the fence. The Dukes lose, eighteen to seventeen.

The team congratulates the Monarchs and heads for the showers. No one says anything when they walk past me. Papa looks sad as he gathers up the equipment. I want to help him, but I go straight to the bus instead, wondering if the church basement is still available for my recital.

"Son," Papa finally says on the quiet ride home, "play somethin' happy." He takes the violin down from the baggage rack and hands it to me. "We could all use a little cheerin' up."

"I . . . I was afraid you wouldn't like my music anymore." I twist the pegs and make sure it's tuned.

"Of course I still like your music," Papa sits in the seat and puts me on his lap. "It sure helped us get a lot further than I thought we could without our best players. Shoot, when I shut my big mouth and listened, I loved what I heard. I love you, though, most of all. Win or lose—Negro Leagues or not—ain't no ball game ever gonna change that."

"I love you, too, Papa." I hug him and then play the "Minute Waltz" over and over again.

A week later, baseball season is over, and at last I perform my recital. The only sound heard through our house on Tyler Road is the softness of a Schubert sonata—with no mistakes. Mama, Papa, the Dukes and their wives fill the first four rows of our crowded living room.

"You folks must be right proud of Reginald," I hear Mr. LaRue whisper. "He sure plays a powerful fiddle."

Papa smiles and puts his arm around Mama. "Sure does," he says, "'cept, we prefer to call it a *violin*."